President Lincoln:
From Log Cabin to White House
© 2016 Demi

Demi and Wisdom Tales would like to extend their appreciation to Dr. James M. Cornelius at the Abraham Lincoln Presidential Library & Museum in Springfield, Illinois for his generous assistance.

Wisdom Tales is an imprint of World Wisdom, Inc.

Library of Congress Cataloging-in-Publication Data
Demi, author.
President Lincoln : from log cabin to White House / Demi.
pages cm
Audience: Age 4-8.
Audience: Grade K to grade 3.
ISBN 978-1-937786-50-2 (casebound : alk. paper) 1. Lincoln, Abraham, 1809-1865--Juvenile literature. 2. Presidents--United States--Biography-- Juvenile literature. I. Title.
E457.905.D454 2016
973.7092--dc23
[B]
2015031969

Printed in China on acid-free paper.

Production Date: September 2015,
Plant & Location: Printed by 1010 Printing International Ltd,
Job/Batch #: TT15080667

For information address Wisdom Tales,
P.O. Box 2682, Bloomington, Indiana 47402-2682
www.wisdomtalespress.com

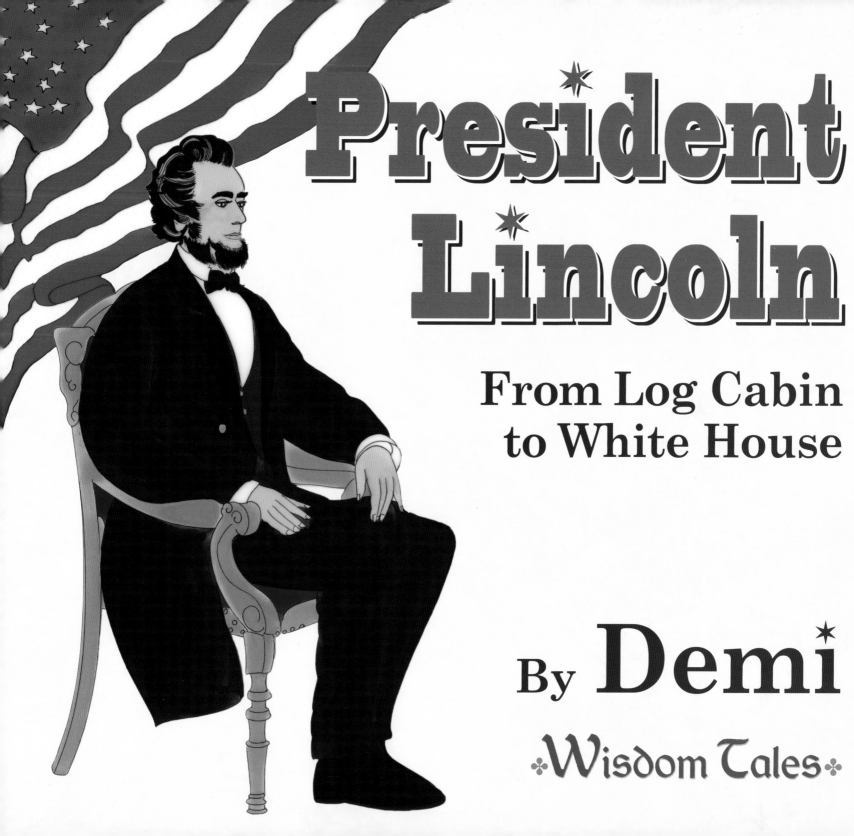

President Lincoln

From Log Cabin to White House

By Demi

Wisdom Tales

Abraham Lincoln was born on February 12, 1809 in a one room log cabin on Sinking Spring Farm, near Hodgenville, Kentucky. His father, Thomas, was a farmer and carpenter and his mother, Nancy, a seamstress.

"*God bless my mother. All that I am or ever hope to be I owe to her.*"—Abraham Lincoln

Abraham's mother couldn't read or write, but she knew parts of the Bible by heart. She would recite these to Abraham and his older sister Sarah. Abraham loved learning and would memorize what he heard.

When Abraham was six, he and Sarah began to go to school.
The students would shout out their ABCs and 123s in order to learn them.
It was very noisy! However, the Lincoln children couldn't always go to school.
They needed to help on the farm. Abraham and Sarah would fetch water,
cut firewood, and plant seeds of corn, beans, pumpkins, and potatoes.

"When first my father settled here,
'Twas then the frontier line:
The panther's scream filled night with fear
And bears preyed on the swine."
—A.L. "The Bear Hunt"

Two years later, the family moved to a forest in Indiana.
They built a new cabin with the help of some relatives.
The woods were full of wolves, bears, and other wild animals.

Because life was so hard then, people often became sick.
Abraham's mother died when he was nine and Sarah was eleven.
The last words she spoke to them were, "Be good and kind to your father—
to one another and to the world. I want you to live as I have taught you."

These were sad days for them. Soon, a good thing happened.
Abraham's father married again one year later.

Abraham's new stepmother, Sarah Bush Johnston, and her three children
came to live with the Lincolns in 1820. She was very kind and warm.
She also brought something very special with her—books!
His stepmother saw that Abraham loved to read.

When Abraham plowed the fields he would let the horses rest at the end of each row. Then he would pull out a book from his shirt and begin reading. Books were hard to find where Abraham lived.

Once, he walked almost twenty miles to borrow a single book.
Another time, the rain stained the cover of a book he had borrowed.
Abraham had to work for three days to pay for the damage.

"Cruelty to animals is wrong. An ant's life is to it, as sweet as ours to us."—A.L.

Abraham also loved animals. One day, he spent a whole afternoon
trying to rescue a little groundhog caught in a rock. He couldn't pull it out.
So, he walked all the way to the blacksmith's shop to borrow a hooked pole.
Returning, he managed to set the poor groundhog free.

When Abraham was nineteen, he was already very tall and strong. He began to work on a boat on the Ohio River and the Mississippi River. On his travels he saw many interesting things. He also saw some things that he didn't like. People were selling African men, women, and children as slaves in a market in New Orleans.

Soon, the Lincoln family moved to a new cabin in Illinois.
Abraham was a man now and went out on his own.
He tried many kinds of work. He dug wells and cut down trees.
He also worked in a store. The customers liked to hear his stories and jokes.
One evening, Abraham saw that he had charged a
customer too much money. It was late at night and
the customer lived many miles away.
Yet, Abraham walked all the way to her house
to return the money.

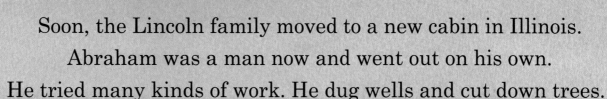

"*Resolve to be honest at all events; and if in your own judgment you cannot be an honest lawyer, resolve to be honest without being a lawyer.*"—A.L.

Abraham finally decided to become a lawyer. He studied law all by himself.
He took the oral law exams and passed. He was twenty-eight years old.
His old habit of learning by reading had given him a new start in life.

A year later, Abraham met Mary Todd at a dance.
She came from a wealthy family. He was a poor lawyer.
Yet Mary saw that Abraham was intelligent, kind, and hard-working.
Abraham and Mary were married in 1842.
He gave her an engraved ring that said, "Love is Eternal."

Almost a year later the Lincolns' first son was born. His name was Robert.
The Lincolns had three more sons, but only Robert lived to become an adult.
So, both joy and sorrow were often parts of the Lincolns' lives.

When Abraham Lincoln was thirty-seven, he was elected to the United States Congress in Washington D.C. Lincoln tried to stop the spread of slavery. After two years as a congressman, he returned to Illinois.

"If slavery is not wrong, nothing is wrong." —A.L.

For a while, Lincoln worked again as a lawyer.
In 1858, he decided to run for a seat
in the United States Senate.
He and his opponent, Stephen Douglas,
had seven famous debates.
Lincoln lost the election, but
many people noticed
and liked him.

*"A house divided against
itself cannot stand."*—A.L.

In 1860, when Lincoln was fifty-one, he was elected President. He told Americans that he was against slavery. Yet, he didn't want America to split into two parts, one that was for slavery and another that was against it.

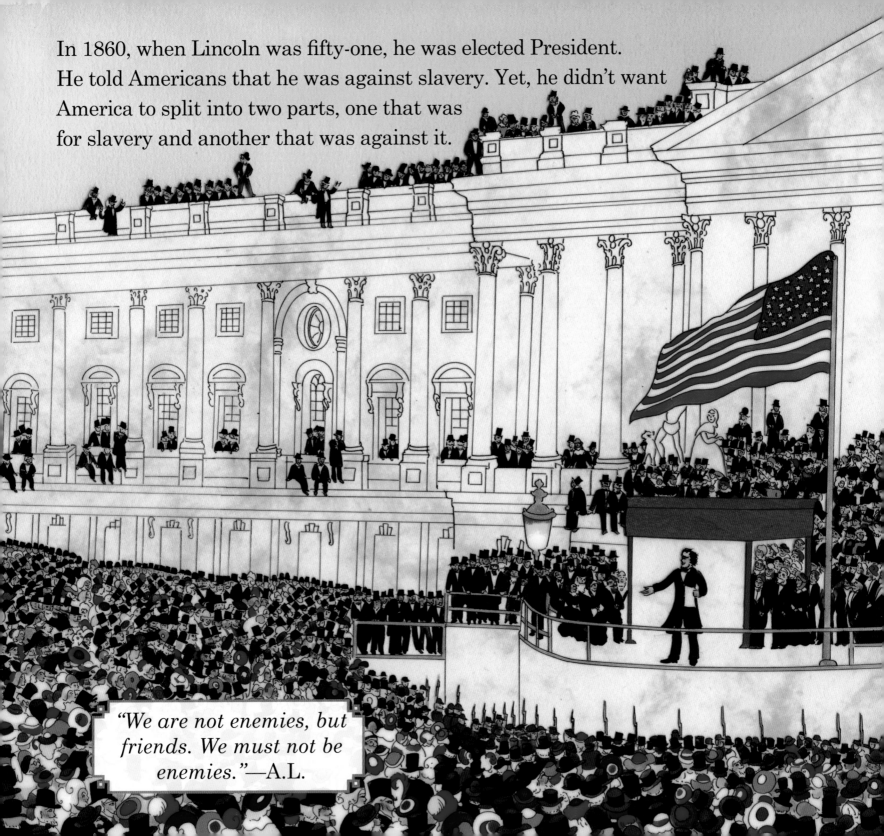

"We are not enemies, but friends. We must not be enemies."—A.L.

Soon, eleven states in the South broke away from the Union to form the Confederacy. On April 12, 1861 Confederate soldiers fired on Fort Sumter in Charleston, South Carolina. This started the American Civil War. Lincoln now faced the most difficult and important job of his life: keeping the great country together. One. Indivisible.

Everyone hoped the Civil War would end quickly, but it did not. Many people were suffering. Yet, Lincoln was grateful to God for the good things He had given. So, on October 3, 1863, Lincoln set a day for everyone to give thanks. Since then, Thanksgiving Day has always been a very important holiday.

Before the war ended, President Lincoln had
declared in the Emancipation Proclamation of January 1, 1863
that all slaves in the states that had broken away
would be free.

"The moment came when I felt that slavery must die that the nation might live!"—A.L.

African-Americans were now able to serve in the Union armed forces. The Massachusetts 54th Regiment was the first African-American regiment to fight in the Civil War. They bravely led the charge in the battle for Fort Wagner, South Carolina. Over 179,000 African-American men served in the Union army and navy during the course of the war.

At Gettysburg, Pennsylvania, Lincoln gave a famous speech. He restated the need for the war and the importance of keeping the country together.

Lincoln was reelected for a second term as president on November 8, 1864. Cheering crowds and military bands greeted him as he returned to office in March 1865.

On April 9, 1865 General Grant and General Lee met at Appomattox, Virginia. After four long years of fighting, the Southern states agreed to free the slaves and rejoin the Union. Yet, Lincoln knew much work lay ahead to rebuild the wounded nation.

Lincoln fought hard for the passage of the 13th Amendment to the Constitution which abolished slavery. It was passed by Congress on January 31, 1865 and finally ratified by enough states on December 6, 1865.

Abraham and Mary Lincoln were happy that the terrible wartimes were over. They went to watch a play one evening. A man named John Wilkes Booth, who was angry that Lincoln wanted to give the vote to African-Americans, killed the President during the play. Abraham Lincoln died on April 15, 1865. He was fifty-six years old. His body traveled by train to Illinois for burial. Between eight to ten million people came to say goodbye.

It is a symbol of courage and freedom. Every year around six million people visit.

The words on the Lincoln Memorial read:

IN THIS TEMPLE, AS IN THE HEARTS OF THE PEOPLE
FOR WHOM HE SAVED THE UNION, THE MEMORY
OF ABRAHAM LINCOLN IS ENSHRINED FOREVER.

From a log cabin to the White House,
Abraham Lincoln traveled far to become
one of America's greatest presidents.
He was full of honesty, wisdom, and compassion.
He also believed that all people are created equal,
and that everyone has the right to be free.
He gave his life to help make this belief come true.

The United States of America in 1861

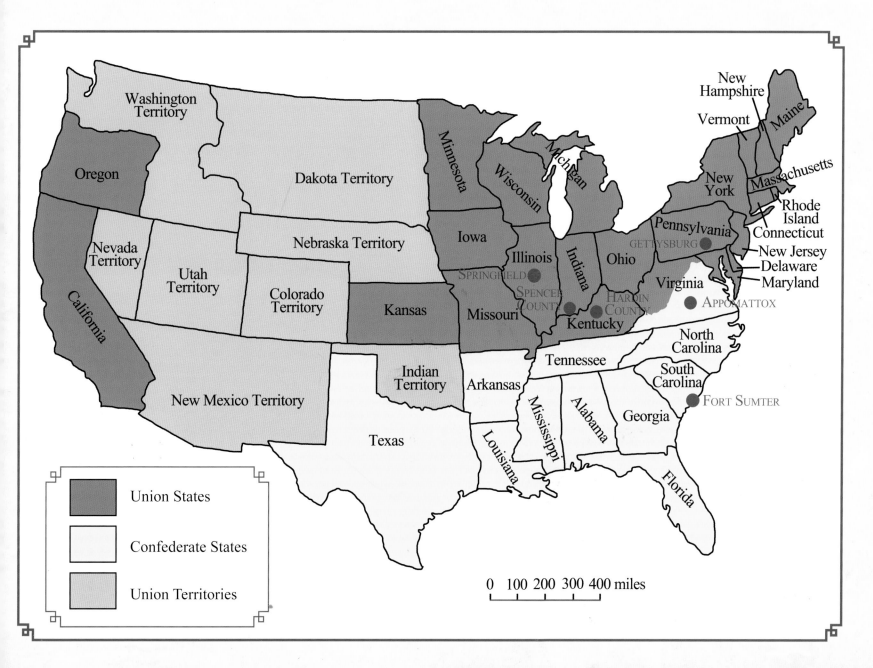

Washington Territory

Oregon

Dakota Territory

Minnesota

Wisconsin

Michigan

New Hampshire

Vermont

Maine

New York

Massachusetts

Nevada Territory

Utah Territory

Nebraska Territory

Iowa

Illinois

Indiana

Ohio

Pennsylvania

GETTYSBURG

Rhode Island

Connecticut

New Jersey

Delaware

Maryland

California

Colorado Territory

Kansas

SPRINGFIELD

SPENCER COUNTY

HARDIN COUNTY

Missouri

Kentucky

Virginia

APPOMATTOX

North Carolina

Tennessee

New Mexico Territory

Indian Territory

Arkansas

Mississippi

Alabama

South Carolina

Georgia

FORT SUMTER

Texas

Louisiana

Florida

Union States

Confederate States

Union Territories

0 100 200 300 400 miles

The Gettysburg Address

Portrait of Abraham Lincoln taken in
November 1863

Four score and seven years ago our fathers brought forth on this continent, a new nation, conceived in Liberty, and dedicated to the proposition that all men are created equal.

Now we are engaged in a great civil war, testing whether that nation, or any nation so conceived and so dedicated, can long endure. We are met on a great battlefield of that war. We have come to dedicate a portion of that field, as a final resting place for those who here gave their lives that that nation might live. It is altogether fitting and proper that we should do this.

But, in a larger sense, we can not dedicate—we can not consecrate— we can not hallow—this ground. The brave men, living and dead, who struggled here, have consecrated it, far above our poor power to add or detract. The world will little note, nor long remember what we say here, but it can never forget what they did here. It is for us the living, rather, to be dedicated here to the unfinished work which they who fought here have thus far so nobly advanced. It is rather for us to be here dedicated to the great task remaining before us—that from these honored dead we take increased devotion to that cause for which they gave the last full measure of devotion— that we here highly resolve that these dead shall not have died in vain—that this nation, under God, shall have a new birth of freedom—and that government of the people, by the people, for the people, shall not perish from the earth.

Abraham Lincoln

November 19, 1863

The Life of President Lincoln

1806 - Lincoln's parents, Thomas Lincoln and Nancy Hanks, marry in Washington County, Kentucky.

1807 - February 10: Lincoln's sister, Sarah, is born in Elizabethtown, Kentucky.

1809 - February 12: Abraham Lincoln is born in a one room log cabin in Hardin County, Kentucky.

1811 - Lincoln family move to another farm in Kentucky on Knob Creek.

1815-16 - Abraham briefly attends school with his sister Sarah.

1816 - Lincoln family settles in Spencer County, Indiana.

1818 - October 5: Lincoln's mother, Nancy, dies and is buried in Spencer County, Indiana.

1819 - Lincoln's father, Thomas, marries a widow, Sarah Bush Johnston, in Elizabethtown, Kentucky.

1820 - Thomas Lincoln returns to Indiana with his new wife and her children, Elizabeth, Matilda, and John.

1828 - January 20: Abraham's sister, Sarah, dies during childbirth.

1830 - Lincoln's family move to Illinois, near Decatur; Abraham delivers his first political speech.

1831-37 - Settles in New Salem, Illinois; works as a boat-builder, store clerk, carpenter, saw-miller, river-pilot, logger, farm helper, and surveyor; serves as a captain and private in the Black Hawk War.

1834 - Elected to the Illinois General Assembly; begins law studies.

1837 - March 1: Lincoln admitted to the Illinois Bar; begins to practice law.

- March 3: Makes first public statement against slavery.

1842 - Marries Mary Todd of Kentucky; they have four sons: Robert, Edward, William, and Thomas; only Robert survives to adulthood.

1846 - Lincoln elected to U.S. Congress; votes in favor of abolition of slavery; opposes Mexican War.

1858 - August 21: Begins first of seven debates against Stephen A. Douglas for Senate position.

- November 2: Loses Senate election to Douglas.

1860 - November 6: Elected as the sixteenth President of the U.S.

1861 - April 12: Attack on Fort Sumter; Civil War begins.

1863 - January 1: Signs the Emancipation Proclamation, freeing slaves in the Southern states.

- October 3: Introduces a national day of Thanksgiving.

- November 19: Delivers the Gettysburg Address.

1864 - April 8: The Thirteenth Amendment, which formally abolishes slavery in the U.S., passed by the Senate.

1865 - March 4: Begins a second term of presidency.

- April 9: Civil War ends with the surrender of the Confederate Army in Appomattox, Virginia.

- April 14-15: Lincoln is shot by actor John Wilkes Booth in Ford's Theatre, Washington; he dies the next morning, aged 56.

- April 21-May 3: Lincoln's body is taken in a funeral train to Springfield, Illinois.

- May 4: Abraham Lincoln is buried in Oak Ridge Cemetery, outside Springfield, Illinois.

1922 - The Lincoln Memorial in Washington, D.C. is built to honor Abraham Lincoln.

Fascinating Facts

Child and Young Man

Abraham Lincoln's formal schooling amounted to around twelve months. Yet, by reading and studying on his own, he gradually learned his way to greatness as a lawyer, orator, statesman, and leader.

When he was young, Abraham had no paper or pencil for studying, so he used charcoal and a wooden shovel as a board. When the surface became full of writing and arithmetic, he would use a knife to shave the surface clean.

Young Abraham had a tender love for animals. At school, he saw some of his classmates put red-hot coals on the back of a helpless turtle. He stopped them, saying that cruelty to animals is wrong.

Abraham was a talented wrestler, losing just twice in many matches. He is listed in the Wrestling Hall of Fame.

Lawyer and Politician

Lincoln the lawyer kept his important papers inside his tall stovepipe hat. Once, some boys played a trick on him by knocking off his hat with a piece of string. Lincoln's papers flew everywhere, but he enjoyed the joke!

When Lincoln was a young lawyer riding in the countryside, he saw two baby birds cast out of their nest. To his friend's surprise, Lincoln picked up the chicks, climbed the tree in his suit, and deposited them back into their nest. "I could not have slept well tonight if I had not saved those birds," he said.

Lincoln wanted women to have the vote in 1836, twelve years before the first women's rights convention and more than eighty years before it became legal.

Lincoln lost five separate elections—for the Illinois General Assembly, for the U.S. Congress, for the U.S. Senate (twice), and as the candidate for vice-president at the 1856 Republican convention. Yet, through perseverance and determination he triumphed over these failures to become the sixteenth president of the U.S. in 1860.

Family Man with Animals

Lincoln's favorite dog, Fido, was the very first presidential pet to be photographed.

When the Lincoln family moved into the White House, the president allowed his sons Tad (Thomas) and Willie (William) to have as many pets as they wanted. There were dogs, cats, weasels, turtles, rabbits, mice, turkeys, horses, and two lively goats named Nanny and Nanko. Tad and Willie would harness the goats to a cart or kitchen chair and have the animals pull them through the White House!

A turkey named Jack received the first presidential pardon after it was sent to the White House for a holiday dinner in 1863. Lincoln's son Tad had grown fond of the turkey and pleaded that it not be killed. President Lincoln agreed and issued "an order of reprieve" sparing Jack the turkey's life. Since then, a ceremony is held each Thanksgiving at which the president of the United States "pardons" a turkey.

about Abraham Lincoln

In one story, Lincoln's cat, Tabby, ate at the White House dinner table. When Mrs. Lincoln remarked to guests, "Don't you think it's shameful for Mr. Lincoln to feed Tabby with a gold fork?" President Lincoln answered: "If the gold fork was good enough for former President James Buchanan, I think it is good enough for Tabby."

President

Lincoln was the first American president to wear a beard. Grace Bedell, an eleven-year-old girl from Westfield, New York, had written Lincoln a letter in 1860 suggesting he grow a beard—and he decided to heed her advice!

Lincoln was the tallest U.S. president at 6'4".

Lincoln was the only president to have a registered patent (no. 6,469). He invented an inflatable bellows device to help steamboats if they ran aground in shallow waters or hit a fallen tree.

Lincoln's most famous speech, the Gettysburg Address, lasted less than three minutes. As photographs in those days needed longer exposures, no photographs of Lincoln's delivery exist.

For Lincoln's burial in Springfield, Illinois, his favorite horse, Old Bob, walked behind the hearse, covered in a black blanket with a silver fringe. His beloved dog, Fido, was also in town to greet the mourners.

Lincoln Yesterday and Today

Today, President Abraham Lincoln's face can be seen on both the penny and five dollar bill, while his face is carved into the southeastern side of Mount Rushmore in South Dakota's Black Hills National Forest.

Lincoln's famous words, "To care for him who shall have borne the battle, and for his widow, and his orphan," flank the entrance to the Washington, D.C. headquarters of the Department of Veterans Affairs (VA), whose task is to care for those injured during war and provide for the families of those who have died in battle.

Famous Quotes from

Personal Description

"If any personal description of me is thought desirable, it may be said, I am, in height, six feet, four inches, nearly; lean in flesh, weighing, on average one hundred and eighty pounds; dark complexion, with coarse black hair and grey eyes—no other marks or brands recollected." (Letter of December 20, 1859)

Education

"A capacity and taste for reading gives access to whatever has already been discovered by others." (Speech of September 30, 1859)

"Get books, sit down anywhere, and go to reading for yourself." (Letter of August 3, 1858)

"Always bear in mind that your own resolution to succeed is more important than any other one thing." (Letter of November 5, 1855)

"It is my pleasure that my children are free, happy, and unrestrained by parental tyranny. Love is the chain whereby to bind a child to its parents." (Remark made when chided or praised for indulging his children, according to Mary Lincoln, 1866)

Virtue

"Do good to those who hate you and turn their ill will to friendship." (Remark to Mary Lincoln, no date)

Abraham Lincoln reading with his son Tad, February 1864

"To His care recommending you, as I hope in your prayers you will recommend me, I bid you an affectionate farewell." (Speech of February 11, 1861)

"Treat him with mercy as he makes the disclosure [of doing wrong] himself." (Letter of November 7, 1864)

"I am a patient man—always willing to forgive on the Christian terms of repentance; and also to give ample *time* for repentance." (Letter of July 26, 1862)

"Bad promises are better broken than kept." (Speech of April 11, 1865)

Work

"Discourage litigation. Persuade your neighbors to compromise whenever you can. Point out to them how

Abraham Lincoln

the nominal winner is often a real loser—in fees, expenses, and waste of time. As a peacemaker the lawyer has a superior opportunity of being a good man. There will still be business enough." (Notes on a law lecture, July 1, 1850)

Slavery

"A house divided against itself cannot stand. I believe this government cannot endure, permanently half *slave* and half *free*. . . . It will become *all* one thing, or *all* the other." (Speech of June 16, 1858)

"There is no reason in the world why the Negro is not entitled to all the natural rights enumerated in the Declaration of Independence, the right to life, liberty, and the pursuit of happiness. I hold that he is as much entitled to these as the white man." (Speech of August 21, 1858)

"The fight must go on. The cause of civil liberty must not be surrendered at the end of *one* or even one *hundred* defeats." (Letter of November 19, 1858)

"He who would *be* no slave, must consent to *have* no slave. Those who deny freedom to others, deserve it not for themselves; and, under a just God, cannot long retain it." (Letter of April 6, 1859)

"If my name ever goes into history, it will be for this act, and my whole soul is in it." (Remark made before signing the final Emancipation Proclamation, January 1, 1863)

"I never in my life felt more certain that I was doing right than I do in signing this [Emancipation Proclamation] paper." (Comment of January 1, 1863)

War

"Sir, my concern is not whether God is on our side; my greatest concern is to be on God's side, for God is always right." (Comment made to an aide during the Civil War, no date)

"Fondly do we hope—fervently do we pray—that this mighty scourge of war may speedily pass away. . . . With malice toward none; with charity for all; with firmness in the right, as God gives us to see the right, let us strive on to finish the work we are in; to bind up the nation's wounds, to care for him who shall have borne the battle, and for his widow, and his orphan—to do all which may achieve and cherish a just and a lasting peace among ourselves, and with all nations." (Second inaugural address, March 4, 1865)

Thanksgiving Day

"I, Abraham Lincoln, President of the United States, do hereby appoint and set apart the last Thursday in November next as a day which I desire to be observed by all my fellow citizens wherever they may then be as a day of Thanksgiving and Praise to Almighty God the beneficent Creator and Ruler of the Universe." (Thanksgiving proclamation, October 20, 1864)

Destiny

"I claim not to have controlled events, but confess plainly that events have controlled me." (Letter of April 4, 1864)